Est 2009

ENTERTAINING READING FOR AN INSPIRATIONAL LAVATORIAL EXPERIENCE

BOG BOOKS

MADE IN GREAT BRITAIN

Ian Bowie and Tim Bulmer, a meeting of two minds...

The scene takes place in the snug of a 17th Century coaching inn somewhere in Old London Town on a rainy day in April...

Ian: Did you draw that?

Tim: I might have

Ian: Fancy a pint?

Tim: Are you buying?

Ian: Only if you drew that

Tim: Then I did

Ian: Then I'm buying

Pause while Ian goes off to get the drinks

Tim: Cheers

Ian: Cheers

Ian: I'm Ian

Tim: Tim

Ian: Are you famous?

Tim: My wife's heard of me

Ian: Good enough for me

Tim: What do you do then?

Ian: I write books

Tim: What sort of books?

Ian: The sort that need pictures. Are you interested?

Tim: Might be

Ian: Fancy some crisps with that?

...and here we are!

A Bog Book Original 2009

Bog Books believe in sourcing locally whenever possible and all our books are printed in Great Britain. We do our best to be as low impact and environmentally friendly as possible but unfortunately some trees were unavoidably killed in the making of this book, sorry.

Layout, design and all the funky clever stuff by Gary & Cheryl-ann at Design Farm, thanks chap and chapette. If you like the look of what you're holding pay them a visit at www.designfarmstudio.co.uk

This book would not have been possible without a meeting of two great creative minds over a couple of beers in Covent Garden. Credit goes to:

Original text   *Ian Bowie*
Funky illustrations *Tim Bulmer*

Keep your eyes open for more Bowie and Bulmer originals from Bog Books.

www.bogbooksltd.co.uk

Contents

 Yorkshire Speak - *A users guide for those who want to know what the bloody hell Yorkshire Folk are talking about!*

Introduction

"Thas nowt sa queer as fowk!" so the saying goes, and Yorkshire folk should know. Traitors, vampires, explorers, adventurers, rockers and rollers, the biggest county in England has been, and in some cases still is, home to some of the queerest folk in the land. If you fancy a pint in the highest pub in England, a wander round the streets of the country's oldest city or a drive along the longest lime tree avenue in Europe, you're in the right county and 'Yorkshire Pudding 'n' All That Tripe' will tell you where to find them, and a lot more to boot.

Yorkshire facts for the uninitiated

Stretching from Scarborough on the East coast to within twelve miles of Morecambe Bay on the West coast, Yorkshire is England's largest county which includes North Yorkshire, West Yorkshire, South Yorkshire and East Yorkshire (formerly Humberside).

There are more acres of land in Yorkshire than letters in the King James Bible.

After Northumberland, Yorkshire has the lowest population density in England with just 74 people per sq, kilometre compared to a national average of 401.

More than 42% of the population lives in settlements of fewer than 3,000 residents.

Within its borders Yorkshire has two of England's nine National Parks - The Yorkshire Dales and North York Moors.

MORECAMBE BAY 12

SCARBOROUGH

The White Rose County

The White Rose as a symbol of Yorkshire is commonly believed to date back to the 14th Century and Edmund of Langley the First Duke of York and founder of the House of York. The rose is symbolic of the Virgin Mary and white is the symbol of light, typifying purity, innocence, joy and glory.

Ow'do - *A favourite form of greeting - can mean hello, good morning or good afternoon. It is non-gender specific and can even be used when greeting the queen. As in, 'Ow'do yer majesty'.*

Yorkshire Day

On August 1st 1759 after the battle of Minden in Germany, soldiers from the King's Own Yorkshire Light Infantry, who had fought in the battle, picked white roses from bushes near to the battlefields and pinned them to their tunics as a tribute to their fallen comrades. Yorkshire day is now held on this date every year.

A brew - Tea. Yorkshire's very own performance enhancer; drunk in place of viagra.

Flying the flag

The Yorkshire flag is a white rose on a light blue background. It was finally entered into the UK Flag Institute's Register of Flags in June 2008. Prior to this, in order to fly the flag, planning permission was needed and a fee of £60 was payable as it was considered advertising rather than a statement of Yorkshire pride. If you dared hoist your flag without permission from the local council you were liable to be prosecuted and fined. But not hung drawn and quartered.

Owt and nowt - *Something and nothing. 'Tha doesn't get owt for nowt'* *Wise advice given to tourists complaining about the prices*

York

York was founded at the junction of the rivers Ouse and Foss by a garrison of 5000 Roman soldiers around AD71. It is said that 'The history of York is the history of England'. An interesting, and for some perhaps, useful bit of history, is that York is the only place left in England where it is still legal to shoot a Scotsman, but only with a bow and arrow and not on a Sunday!

Jammy - Lucky. As in, 'Jammy bugger' a pseudonym for National Lottery Winner.

Let the train take the strain

If you don't fancy hiking across the moors but still want to experience the spectacular scenery the North Yorkshire Moors Railway have just the ticket you need. It's all aboard at Pickering before setting off back in time to the 1912 themed Levisham station right out on the moors proper. The train puffs on through Newton Dale to Goathland which doubled for Aidensfield station in 'Heartbeat' and is probably better known to Potter fans as 'Hogsmeade' in the film 'Harry Potter and the Philosopher's Stone'. And if being close to all that celebrity excitement made you thirsty there's a chance to refresh yourself in the tea-room at Grosmont before the final leg of the journey down to Whitby and a quick bite in Dracula's favourite seaside resort. So sit back, relax and let the train take the strain.

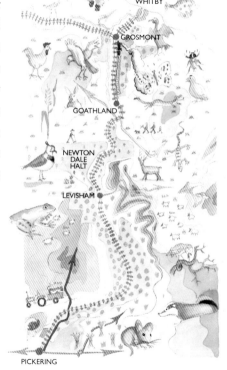

Gormless - *Witless. Anyone not from Yorkshire.*

Pickering...Levisham...Newton Dale Halt...Goathland...Grosmont...Whitby

Sir Nigel Gresley

War Weekend

Volunteers

"Ee -I'm fair Jiggered!"

Richmond Castle

Founded in 1071 by Alan the Red, a Norman lord under William 1, Richmond castle is the oldest surviving stone castle in England. If you visit the castle and 'scout' about a bit you will discover a plaque set into the wall near the Southwest corner commemorating the fact Lord Baden-Powell resided in the castle from 1908-1910.

Jiggered - Tired. A feeling, commonly associated with a long stint on the bog. As in, 'Ee I'm rite jiggered' after that.

" Be prepared ! "

What's in a name?

With 27 letters the village of Sutton-under-Whitestonecliffe, in North Yorkshire, is the longest single-word place-name in England. Don't forget your wide-angled lens if you want to take your picture standing next to the village sign.

Aye - *Yes. A form of consent popular at weddings 'Do you, Norman Clegghorn, take Mary Higginbottom to be your lawful wedded wife?' 'Aye'.*

Londesborough and the saving of Yorkshire

Depending on your interest in religion the small village of Londesborough might be worthy of note. For it was here in 627 A.D. that King Edwin of Northumberland was, for better or for worse, persuaded by Bishop Paulinus (later Archbishop of York and eventually St. Paulinus) to give up his pagan beliefs and embrace the Christian faith. The King was baptized in York on the 12th April 627 so saving the good people of Yorkshire from an eternal fate of hell-fire and damnation, or so he thought.

Pop - *Fizzy drink. Yorkshire Champagne.*

Religious conversion - the gentle art of persuasion !

Whitby

Immortalised in Bram Stoker's Dracula, Whitby is the Yorkshire coastal town where the blood-sucker first set foot on English soil. These days if you fancy a bite you might be better off trying one of the local chip shops. These include The Magpie Fish and Chip restaurant, which according to Rick Stein, serves up the best fish and chips in Britain.

Bray - Beat. Something you do to the batter when making Yorkshire pudding. 'Bray it properly otherwise it wont rise'.

Ripon

Ripon was granted a Royal Charter back in 886 by King Alfred the Great making it Britain's oldest city. The earliest free-standing obelisk in the country can also be found in Ripon market square. The square was described by Daniel Defoe as 'The finest and most beautiful square that is to be seen of its kind in England' and the weekly Thursday market, started in 1292, is still held today.

Bog - *Toilet/Loo. A place for quiet reflection and inspired thought, a sacred place for all Yorkshiremen.*

Stamford Bridge 1066

Of course for most 1066 is synonymous with the Battle of Hastings, but there was an earlier battle in this fateful year. The Battle of Stamford Bridge took place on the 25th September 1066 three weeks before Hastings. It was here, after a four-day forced march, that King Harold Godwinson's forces fought and defeated the invading Norwegian army under King Harald Hardräde. Harold's subsequent defeat at the Battle of Hastings is largely attributed to his army being exhausted from this campaign just a few weeks earlier; but that's not Yorkshire's fault.

Bairns - *Child. Little thing with short legs and a big mouth. Usually travel in groups and terrify adults.*

Rudston

Why should a village with a mere population of just under 400 souls be of interest to anyone? Well if you're a paleontologist, or just like big rocks, then this one should definitely be of interest. Rudston is home to the 25ft (7.6 metre) high Rudston Monolith, the highest standing stone in England. By gum lad, she's a big un!

Cack-handed - *Clumsy. Rugby term for someone who constantly drops the ball.*

The Rhubarb Triangle

The 9 square mile area in West Yorkshire bordered by Wakefield, Morley and Rothwell was at one time responsible for producing 90% of the world's winter rhubarb crop. If rhubarb is your thing then head for Wakefield in February and the festival of food, drink and rhubarb, add some custard and get stuck in.

Snicket - *Alleyway. Common dog-shit trap for the unwary.*

Pub crawl

Yorkshire is home to many great pubs including England's highest, Tan Hill at 1,732 feet above sea level, and also England's oldest Inn, The Bingley Arms at Bardsey which opened for business in 905 AD.

Chuddy - *Chewing-gum. Can be used instead of toothpaste and often found on the sole of your shoe.*

Waiting for service since 905 AD !

Bridge ower nowt

If crossing bridges is one of your things or you just like the unusual and value the unique, head for the village of Sinnington in North Yorkshire. For this is where you can cross a bridge, not over 'troubled water', but over nothing at all. Before leaving don't forget to marvel at the world's first stainless steel maypole too.

Clout - Hit. *What you get when you're cheeky to a lady from Yorkshire.*

The Petrifying Well

Located in Knaresborough and part of the Mother Shipton Estate, England's oldest visitor attraction first opened in 1630! The water has an extremely high mineral content which means everything in its path eventually turns to stone. Don't worry though, this doesn't happen instantaneously. The petrification process depends on the material. Non-porous materials can take up to 18 months so you don't have to worry about dipping your finger in.

Clemmed - Starving. What every restaurant, café and chip shop hopes to welcome – clemmed customers desperate for scran.

Too long in the shower !

Coal face

No book about Yorkshire would be complete without some mention of the county's coal mining heritage. Britain's oldest coal-mine was the Prince of Wales colliery at Pontefract, West Yorkshire. The pit was opened in 1860 and sadly closed in 2002. If you want to find out more about England's coal mining history then visit the National Coal Mining Museum for England at Overton near Wakefield.

Fratch - *Fight. What the kids do on the back seat of the car all the way up the motorway until of course they get to Yorkshire and are so wowed by the scenery they simply gawp in awed silence.*

City of Steel

Yes, Sheffield is famous for its steel and has been since the days of Chaucer who mentioned a 'Sheffield whittle' (a small knife) in The Canterbury Tales way back in the 14th Century. However Sheffield has another claim to fame. With a population of around 500,000 and 2 million trees Sheffield has more trees per capita than any other city in Europe, possibly making it the greenest city in Europe too.

Faffin - *Undecided. What you are accused of when you can't decide whether to have mushy peas or a pickled egg with your fish and chips. As in, 'Come on, stop faffin and make your mind up'.*

Oh Fat Betty

If you hear of someone looking for Fat Betty there's no need to join them in the hunt, call the police, or the local dog-catcher. They are probably tourists, and the Fat Betty in question is the white stone cross to be found on the North York Moors just north of the road from Blakey Rigg to Rosedale Abbey. At least it should be; apologies to any Fat Betty that might truly be lost.

Sarnies - *Sandwiches. Survival rations for hikers and walkers.*

On Ilkla Moor baht 'at

As well as providing the inspiration for Yorkshire's unofficial anthem Ilkley Moor has been visited by aliens. In 1987 retired policeman Phillip Spencer got a photograph of one out on the moor before the slippery devil escaped in his UFO. Keep your eyes peeled, there might be more aliens in Yorkshire than you think.

Flippin'eck - *Exclamation of surprise or disappointment. Usually uttered by supporters of the losing team at rugby, cricket and football matches.*

Dale hopping

You've heard about them, you've probably tried to catch mice using cheese from one of them, but how many of them have you actually visited? The Yorkshire Dales are famous throughout the world and renowned for their breathtaking natural beauty. But if you really want to 'do the Dales' then you'll have sixteen to visit in total. The list, in alphabetical order, is as follows:

Arkengarthdale, Birkdale, Bishopdale, Chapel-Le-Dale, Coverdale, Dentdale, Garsdale, Langstrothdale, Littondale, Kingsdale, Malhamdale, Nidderdale, Ribblesdale, Swaledale, Wensleydale and Wharfedale.

Flummoxed - Confused. Something tourists get when jokers move the road signs.

Doing the Dales

Yorkshire Grub

Time for pudding

The first known Yorkshire Pudding recipe was published in 1737 in 'The Whole Duty of a Woman' and was called 'A Dripping Pudding'. It caught on and since 2008, when the first one was held, Yorkshire Pudding Day is celebrated on February 3rd.

Gander - Look at. Part of the mating ritual at parties. As in, 'Ee-by-gum, 'ave a gander at that'.

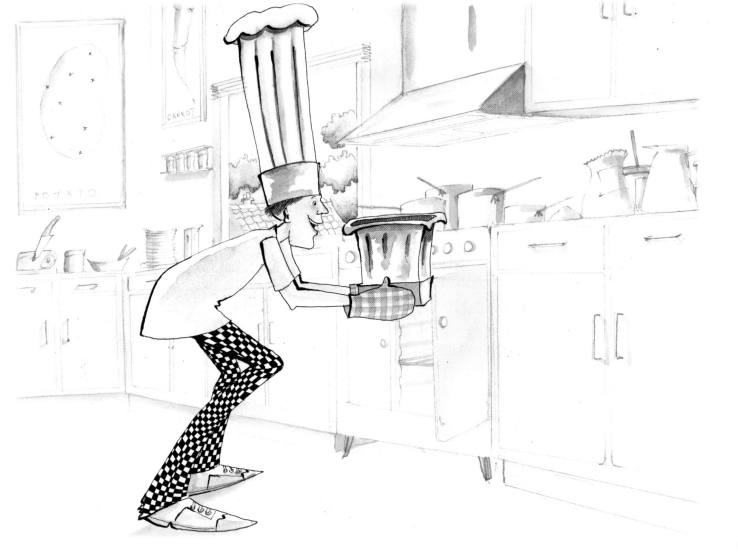

All that tripe

Why on earth would anyone want to eat the stomach lining of a cow? Because they can perhaps? A trip to Yorkshire would not be complete without a plate of tripe and onions. As the saying goes; 'what doesn't kill you will only make you stronger', or is that just a load of old tripe?

Guff - *Fart. When the dog gets blamed for doing what Grandma does.*

Cheese please

If you happen to find yourself in Wensleydale, Swaledale or Ribbledale you might be forgiven for thinking Yorkshire smells a bit cheesey. Not surprisingly, as these three dales have all lent their names to local cheeses. Don't forget the crackers!

 Trump - *Another fart. Something better done on the bog unless you're in a long-term relationship.*

Have a chip

Although the first chip in Britain was fried in Oldham, Lancashire, around 1860, there is actually a chippy in Yeadon, a borough of Leeds, that calls itself 'The Oldest Fish and Chip Shop in the World'. The biggest chippy in the world is also in Yorkshire. Harry Ramsden's, founded in 1928 in Guisley. It seats over 250 diners and comes complete with oak paneling, wall to wall carpets, crystal chandeliers and stained glass windows. Pass the vinegar!

Gi'over - *Stop it. What you say when you don't believe it's your round again.*

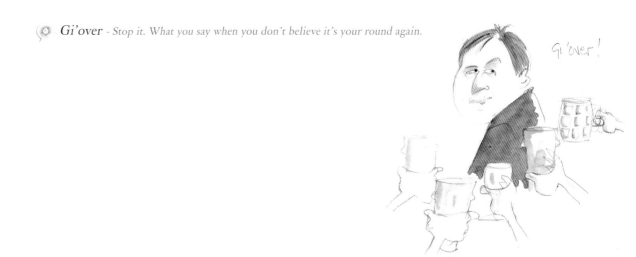

Gi'over!

Near perfection with a delicate, crisp outer layer then I experience the pure joy of that tender heart the potato chip

Ee Pie Gum!

If you like pie then Denby is the place for you. Many hundreds of years ago this small village decided to commemorate special national occasions by baking pies. The very first Denby Dale pie was made in 1788 to celebrate King George III's recovery from madness. What's so special about that you might ask? The answer lies in the size and Denby pies are BIG. Pies have been made to celebrate all sorts of things over the years but the mother of all pies was made in 1988, the bicentenary of the first pie. It contained 3000kgs of English beef, 3000kgs of potatoes and 700kgs of onions. Intended to feed 50,000 people, it was recorded by the Guinness Book of Records as the biggest meat and potato pie in the world.

Chuffed - *Pleased. That happy feeling when it's someone else's round.*

Ale

Yorkshire folk are known for liking their ale and so it should come as no surprise to learn that the beer pump was invented by a Yorkshireman, Joseph Bramah of Stainborough in 1797. If you like a good pint then you will be pleased to know there are a wealth of independent breweries throughout the county ensuring there is always a good reason to take a beer break. And if you ask anyone in Yorkshire for the time they will invariably tell you it's 'beer o'clock'.

Scran - *Food. Basically anything edible, including juicy tourists.*

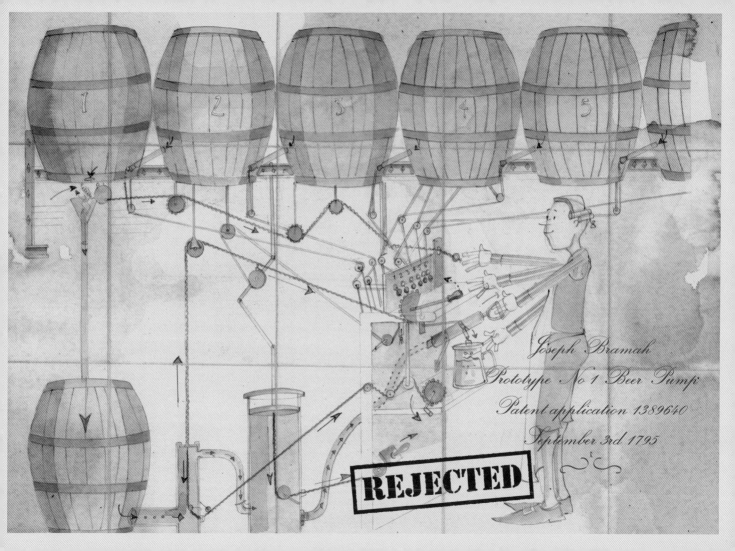

Joseph Bramah

Prototype No 1 Beer Pump

Patent application 1389640

September 3rd 1795

REJECTED

Highway robbery

Probably England's most infamous highwayman, Dick Turpin, real name John Palmer, was hanged in York on Saturday 7th April 1739. He is buried in St. George's churchyard where his grave is marked by a modest headstone. However Turpin was preceded by Yorkshire's very own home-grown highwayman, William Nevison. Born at Pomfret around 1639 Nevison was a colourful 17th Century character plying his dubious trade on the highways and byways of England. Legend has it Charles II nicknamed him 'Swift Nick' after he committed a robbery in London and managed to get back to York the same day in order to supply himself with an alibi. Unfortunately Nick was not swift enough and the law eventually caught up with him. He was hanged at York Castle on 4th May 1685.

Ay up - Hello. Synonym for 'Ow do'.

Remember Remember

Guy Fawkes was born in York in 1570, a true son of Yorkshire. Unfortunately he got involved with the wrong crowd down South and was caught red handed trying to blow up King James 1 during the state opening of parliament on 5th November 1605. Sadly he was not treated to the warm Yorkshire welcome he was used to back home. Instead, he was sentenced to be hung drawn and quartered for his act of treason. Nevertheless, the hapless Fawkes avoided the painful process of having his innards pulled out in front of his dying eyes by managing to jump from the gallows, breaking his own neck.

Bins - Spectacles. Useful map reading device for finding all those interesting places in Yorkshire.

Yorkshire prophet

Ursula Sonthein was born in a cave in Yorkshire in 1488 and became one of the greatest prophets Britain has ever had. "Ursula who?" you might be wondering. Well, at the age of 24 she married a lucky chap called Toby Shipton and became a respected healer and fortune-teller and was given the respectful title of 'Mother' Shipton. Amongst other things she is said to have foretold of the Great Fire of London of 1666, the invention of the motorcar and iron ships.

Bits - *Testicles. Integral part of the male body often kept in a box by Yorkshire wives.*

Hasn't she done well !

The Hornblower

As mentioned earlier King Alfred the Great granted Ripon a Royal Charter back in 886. Being a generous fellow the King also offered the good folk a horn as a symbol of the event. To ensure they were not overrun by thieves, murderers and vagabonds during the night the people of Ripon decided to appoint a Wakeman (watchman) to protect them. The horn was to be sounded every night at nine o'clock at the obelisk in the market square to let the citizens know the watch was set and the Wakeman was on patrol. The ritual is still carried out today and has not been missed for one single night in over 1100 years.

Champion!

Champion - *Thank you. To be used when someone offers to buy you a drink. As in, 'That'll be champion'.*

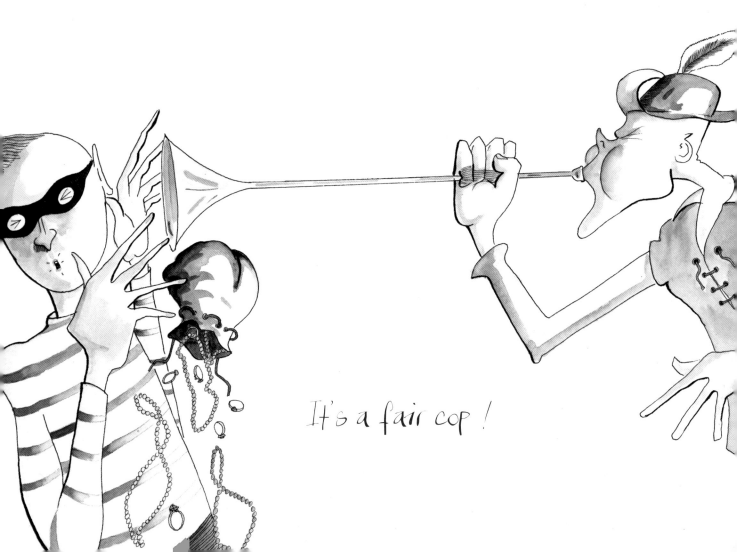

Fine furniture

Yes, Yorkshire is also responsible for giving the world some of its finest pieces of furniture; Master furniture maker Thomas Chippendale was born in Otley in 1718. Chippendale was also the first cabinet-maker to publish a book of his own designs; 'The Gentleman and Cabinet Makers Director' first published in 1754.

Chippendale isn't the only great furniture maker to come from Yorkshire though. If you think you have a mouse in your house you may well be right. Hopefully though it is in the form of the little wooden mouse Robert Thompson of Kilburn used as his signature and trademark and carved into the beautiful Oak furniture he created in the first half of the 20th Century. 'Mouseman' oak furniture is still produced in Kilburn today, by 'Robert Thompson Craftsmen Ltd'.

In the dumps - *Depressed. Low miserable feeling when you have to leave Yorkshire.*

Redoubtable Resolution and Endless Endeavour

Captain James Cook was born in the village of Marton on 7th November 1728. Cook achieved numerous firsts during his lifetime including being the first person to map the Newfoundland coast, make the first European contacts with the Eastern coast of Australia and Hawaiian Islands and make the first recorded circumnavigation of New Zealand.

Pop your clogs - *Die. Something you hope will not happen too soon and when it does that it is in Yorkshire.*

Journalist - *"What inspired you to circumnavigate the globe? Discover new lands, and encounter as yet so many unfamiliar peoples and cultures?"*

Capt Cook - *"Have you met the wife?"*

The Yorkshire giant

Tha breed em big in Yorkshire! William Bradley was born in Market Weighton in the East Riding of Yorkshire on 10th February 1787. By the time he was 20 years old William was 7 feet 9 inches tall and is still today the tallest recorded Englishman ever.

Ee-by-gum - *Oh my God. A form of praise, amazement or trepidation - often uttered by fair maidens when observing, for the first time, the Yorkshire member.*

High flyers

Born on 1st July 1903 in Kingston Upon Hull, Amy Johnson was a true high flyer. Taking off from Croydon on 5th of May 1930 in a De Havilland Gipsy Moth, she became the first woman to fly solo from Britain to Australia landing in Darwin on 24th May after an 11,000 mile flight. Amy wasn't Yorkshire's first high-flyer however. That honour must surely go to 'the father of aerodynamics' Sir George Cayley 6th Baronet of Brompton Hall. A pioneer of aeronautical engineering Cayley designed a manned glider that flew across Brompton Dale in 1853; the first successful manned flight the world had seen. The 150th anniversary of the flight was commemorated by Sir Richard Branson on Saturday 5th July 2003 when he took to the air in a replica of the original glider.

Gumption - *Common sense. Something Yorkshire people have in abundance but no one else seems to possess.*

Cats' Eyes

You know those reflective thingys in the middle of roads in the UK? That's right, cats' eyes, as they are commonly known. Well guess what? Correct, they were invented by a Yorkshireman, Percy Shaw from Halifax who patented his invention in 1934. As James May of Top Gear fame says "The Catseye is what great design is all about. Simple, functional, and beautiful. And on top of that, this little block of iron and rubber has probably done more to save lives on the road than anything since." Hooray for Percy!

Moither - *Bother or disturb. Yorkshire folk are a laid back lot and don't like to be harassed. As in, 'Don't moither me when I'm on the bog'.*

To boldly go where no Yorkshire woman has gone before

They say people from Yorkshire are practical, down to earth and have their feet planted firmly on the ground; but there are exceptions. On the 25th November 1989 former chocolate technologist, Helen Sharman, from Sheffield, beat more than 13,000 other applicants to eventually become Britain's first cosmonaut. She became the first Briton in space on 18th May 1991 spending 8 days on the Mir space station as part of the Soyuz TM-12 mission.

Mithered - *Be bothered. There's no need to rush when in Yorkshire and you will often hear someone say 'I can't be mithered, it can wait 'til tomorrow'.*

Sweet tooth

If you have a sweet tooth and a liking for liquorice then you might be interested to learn that the first liquorice confectionary was invented when George Dunhill added sugar to it in 1760. The Dunhill family grew liquorice in the Pontefract area and so this simple addition to a plant that was probably introduced to Britain by the Romans heralded the birth of the famous Pontefract cake.

Skint - *Broke/without money. If you bet on the wrong horse you might end up skint. If this should happen to you please go to Lancashire.*

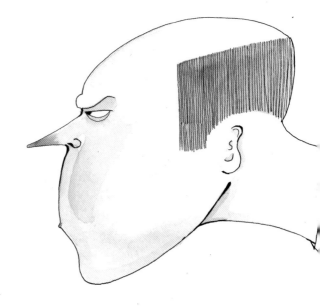

Who's eaten all the Pontefract cakes?

Football world firsts

Yorkshire is officially recognised by FIFA as being the birthplace of club football. The world's oldest football club playing Association football is Sheffield Football Club (not to be confused with Sheffield United or Sheffield Wednesday) founded in 1857. And the world's oldest football ground is Sandygate Road in Sheffield which first opened in 1804 and is home to Hallam FC. This is also where the world's first inter-club match was played on 26th December 1860 between Hallam FC and Sheffield FC. And if all this history wasn't enough there is even a street called Football, in Yeadon near Leeds. It shouldn't be too difficult to find, just look for a house with a dirty great football painted on its end wall.

Sup - A style of drinking born from years of enjoying Ale. As in, 'Don't just drink it lad, sup it'.

Lost Man - *"Could you tell me how to find Football, Yeadon young man?"*

Cheeky Young Yeadonite - *"Are thi blind mister?"*

County champions

Yorkshire County Cricket Club is the most decorated county cricket club in the land. At the time of writing it has won 30 championship titles, 12 more than any other county. Some of England's greatest cricketers also hail from Yorkshire including Len Hutton, Fred Trueman and Geoffrey Boycott. Yorkshire can even claim responsibility for what is probably the most famous cricket ground in the world, 'Lords'. The ground is named after its founder, 'Thomas Lord', who was born in Thirsk on the 23rd November 1755.

Keks - *Trousers. Item of clothing traditionally held up with braces. As in, 'Get yer keks on we're going down the pub.'*

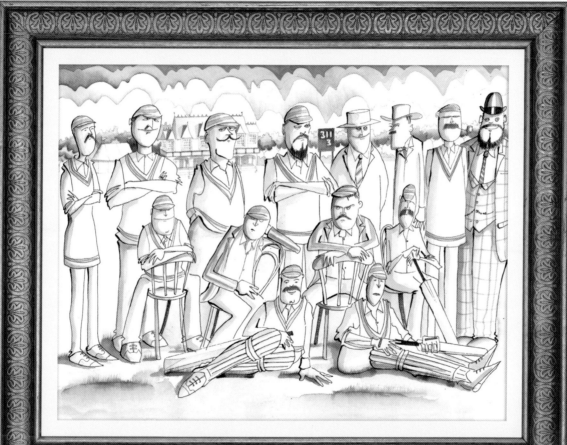

Horses for courses

Traditionally run over 4 miles on the third Thursday in March at Kiplingcotes near Market Weighton. the Kiplingcotes Derby was started in 1519 and is England's oldest flat race.

Gawpin - *Look at with open mouth. Often asked in pubs. As in, 'What're you gawpin at?' The correct and safe answer is 'Nowt'.*

Run foxy run

Not a good county if you're a fox. England's oldest fox hunt is the Bilsdale Hunt established in 1668 by George Villiers the then Duke of Buckingham.

caught fugglin'!

Fugglin - *Cheating. Something never done by the honest residents of Yorkshire. If you're caught fugglin you're likely to get your bits chopped off.*

Rugby League

The Northern Rugby Football Union was formed at the George Hotel in Huddersfield on 29th August 1895. The Union was the result of a break away from the Rugby Football Union by Northern clubs due to a series of disagreements with their counterparts in the South. As every true Yorkshireman knows; 'Tha can't trust them bloody Southerners!' The initial 22 member clubs were soon joined by many more and within fifteen years of this first meeting the new league had over 200 teams.

oooh. me blebs!

Bleb - Blister. Something hikers get on their feet. Not as unpleasant but certainly more painful than a cow pat. As in, 'Looks like we'll have to lance that bleb for you.'

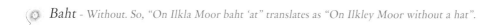

Home of film

If you thought Hollywood gave the world the motion picture you'd be wrong; it was Yorkshire. Yes, the world's first sequence of moving pictures were actually filmed in the grounds of Roundhay Park in Leeds in October 1888 by Frenchman Louis Le Prince.

 Baht - *Without. So, "On Ilkla Moor baht 'at" translates as "On Ilkley Moor without a hat".*

Last of the Summer Wine

An every day tale of Yorkshire folk enjoying the autumn of their years. The first episode of Last of the Summer Wine aired on British television at 8pm on Thursday 4th January 1973. Filmed on location in and around the town of Holmfirth there have been over 30 series to date making this the longest running sitcom in the world.

Causey - *Pavement. Try to stay on it unless you want to be run over.*

Literary figures

Yorkshire was home to Anne, Charlotte and Emily. The Brontë sisters were born in Thornton, Bradford and later moved to Haworth where the surrounding scenery provided inspiration for many of their works. Carrying on the literary tradition playwrights Alan Ayckbourn and Alan Bennett are also sons of Yorkshire.

Chunter - *A form of unclear speech. Often used when you don't want the wife to hear. As in, 'Stop yer chunterin' and speak up.'*

Stars in his eyes

Following in the footsteps of Cook, Patrick Stewart left fair Yorkshire to explore the depths and dangers, not of our world, but of outer space. Born on the 13th July 1940 in Mirfield West Yorkshire, Patrick changed his name to Jean-Luc Picard, and became commander of the most famous star ship of them all, the USS Enterprise. Yes, he's Yorkshire's very own star trekker.

Lark - Have fun. As in, 'You're bound to have a lark in Yorkshire.'

Should it happen to a vet?

James Alfred Wight, perhaps better known as James Herriot, is also responsible for quite a few of the tourists wandering around the Yorkshire Dales. If you are one of them and are looking for 'Darrowby', the fictional town in the BBC TV series 'All Creatures Great and Small', then you need to get yourself to Askrigg which provided the location. Incidentally, Askrigg means 'Ridge with Ash Trees'. You always wanted to know that didn't you?

Mardy - Spoilt kids. As in, 'If you don't bring em up rite thal end up wi mardy young uns.'

Film fans

Over the years Yorkshire has provided the locations for many films including; The Full Monty, Calendar Girls, Brassed Off, Little Voice, Brideshead Revisited and Damned United. Harry Potter fans might also be interested in knowing (nobody else is) that the train sequences in 'Harry Potter and the Philosophers Stone' were filmed on the North Yorkshire Moors Railway. Of greater interest perhaps is the longest lime tree avenue in Europe, found on the drive up to Castle Howard, the location for Brideshead Revisited.

Rue - *Regret. Life can be full of regrets but one thing is sure, you'll rue the day you have to leave Yorkshire.*

Rock and Roll

Yes, Yorkshire rocks and it can sing too! Joe Cocker, Kiki Dee, Robert Palmer, Chris Rea, Tasmin Archer, Arctic Monkeys, Smokie, White Snake, Saxon and Def Leppard are all from Yorkshire. And there are many more!

Feckless - *Useless. Often considered a synonym for husband by many Yorkshire women folk.*

" Sex and Drugs and Rock and Roll and Fish and Chips
and Mushy Peas, some scraps, a slice and a cup of tea..."

Tuff Luv World Tour '84 Town Hall, Batley

Yorkshire Air Ambulance

It may surprise you to know that the Yorkshire Air Ambulance is an independent charity that relies on the generosity of individuals and organisations to help save lives across Yorkshire. As a rapid response air emergency service the charity serves a population of approximately 5 million people across 4 million acres. YAA operate two MD902 Explorer helicopters, G-SASH and G-CEMS from Leeds Bradford International Airport and Sheffield Business Park and together both air ambulances cover the whole of the region and can reach speeds of up to 160 mph. On average, when a patient has been received by the YAA, they will always be only 10 minutes from the nearest hospital and 15 minutes from the most relevant treatment centre, this saves lives. To keep providing this life saving service the charity needs to raise £7200 per day to keep both of Yorkshire's Air Ambulances maintained and in the air. The work of the Yorkshire Air Ambulance has also been documented by the BBC series, 'Helicopter Heroes'.

Bog Books have hooked up with the friendly folk at Yorkshire Air Ambulance to help support the magnificent work they do for the county of Yorkshire. Whether it's a fall on the moors or an accident in the Dales, no matter where the person comes from (even Lancashire) the Yorkshire Air Ambulance will lift-off 7 days a week, 365 days a year, dedicated to saving lives whenever they fly.

In buying this book you are helping to keep the whirlybirds in the air for which we all thank you. Bog Books make a donation from the profits of the sale of every single 'Yorkshire Pudding 'n' All That Tripe' Bog Book to the charity so thank you very much for buying this copy, you've helped them to help save someone's life. To find out more about this life saving service please visit **www.yaa.org.uk**

I ♥ yaa!

About the author

Ian should have been born in Yorkshire but by a strange quirk of fate was lifted kicking and screaming into the Cold War world of 1965 in Carlisle, Cumbria. An English teacher for twenty years Ian had an epiphany while sitting on the bog one day and the rest, as Tim would say, is history.

About the artist

Tim first encountered favourable criticism for his artwork at the age of six when at Wentworth C of E Primary school (near Rotherham). He then entered a cultural void only seeing the sunlight in 1978 when he entered the foundation course at Teeside College of Art. Thirty years later he met Ian and the rest, as they say, is history. (I said the history bit first, not Ian!)

Beyond your Bog Book

If you enjoyed this book why not have a look at the others you can add to your 'Bog Books' collection and also keep up to date with all the latest news and what's going on here at Bog Books HQ by visiting our website **www.bogbooksltd.co.uk**

The website also gives you an opportunity to buy giclée prints of any and all the illustrations from every Bog Book to bring some colour to your bog, or any other room for that matter.

All open edition giclée prints are signed by the artist Tim Bulmer and are a perfect gift for a special someone or a nice treat just for yourself, why not?

Bog Books make a donation from the profits of each 'Yorkshire Pudding 'n' All That Tripe' giclée print and from each Bog Books 'Yorkshire Map' giclée print to the Yorkshire Air Ambulance Charity.

We hope this unique lavatorial experience was an enjoyable one!

Catch you soon, The Bog Book Brigade.

Publishers Information and stuff

First published in 2009 by Bog Books Ltd - www.bogbooksltd.co.uk

Bog Books™ is a Registered Trademark of Bog Books Ltd

ISBN: 978 952 67178 1 4

Designed & Printed in Yorkshire, Great Britain